True Concessions

Also by Craig Poile

First Crack

Craig Poile

True
Concessions

GOOSE LANE

Edited by Jeffery Donaldson.
Cover illustration: Veer.
Cover and interior page design by Julie Scriver.
Printed in Canada on 100% PCW paper.
10 9 8 7 6 5 4 3 2 1

Library and Archives Canada Cataloguing in Publication

Poile, Craig A. (Craig Alexander), 1967-
    True concessions / Craig Poile.

Poems.
ISBN 978-0-86492-530-5

    I. Title.
PS8581.O227T78 2009   C811'.54   C2008-907200-6

Goose Lane Editions acknowledges the financial support of the Canada Council for the Arts, the Government of Canada through the Book Publishing Industry Development Program (BPIDP), and the New Brunswick Department of Wellness, Culture, and Sport for its publishing activities.

Goose Lane Editions
Suite 330, 500 Beaverbrook Court
Fredericton, New Brunswick
CANADA E3B 5X4
www.gooselane.com

For Christopher, Lily & Sam, for bearing with

Contents

Part 1

Candyman

Wheeled out on the grass, a stall
Striped pink and blue, trimmed with
Bulbs that dimly flash in sunlight.
He's alone inside, half-reclined among
Goods variously shaped and dyed,
Bagged and strung up, piled against glass.
Come closer, you get wind of the smell
That answered Hansel's hunger,
Turns stones leading home to crumbs.

Unlike the women over by the funhouse
Who chat and bustle in their Sugar Shack,
He spends his shift bored and starved
For the midway, where his slack clothes,
Their worked-over blue, recharge their scent
Of diesel and grease, soak up the lax sweat
That gathers while he smokes and times the ride,
Tapping to the music, the spit and chug,
As it manufactures joy and panic.

But for now the sugar has settled
On the beard he's trained to his jaw,
The bleached strands that lace his hair,
The creases of tanned knuckles
That dip and twirl the paper cone.
It clings to the coins passed
Between us: a flavour on my thumb
That's sweeter tasted second-hand.

Pegged

The last time I ever, or remember I ever,
Sat drinking the whole afternoon
Was in a Montreal bar, settled over
A red-and-white cloth ringed with stains,

Giving a face to arguments induced
By low wattage, no service, and cheap draft.
My friend had picked the place mostly
So we could brag about where we'd been.

Him I remember for dancing with flowers,
Like Morrissey (he'd read it in a magazine).
He was dreamy and mutinous, betrayed
A mild fixation with the female anus.

We drank and named each table for its tribe:
Folk acts and artists, left-wing hobbyists,
Bombed academics, granola, gay.
And us? Just students, though slow to learn.

When chat turned to the sexual, the tone
Got wound up, self-conscious, tense.
My summer's doings were still a sore topic
Thanks to one blistering night in a tent.

The beer was good (the brand, I think, Black Label),
Each portion fitting neatly into one of
The myriad tabletop "O"s: so many
Glasses filled, that wasted afternoon.

The Dance

The watcher spots an odd, tall bird
Back away from the dance floor, spun
Into a side hall stained by coloured light.
The walls thump with music that moves no one.

She seems tense: neck scarfed, lips smothered,
Ears pinched by charms. A pillbox hat tries
To cover her head. Her tits are strapped
In and wrapped, like little black mummies.

His smile only widens when he sees
It's me, a friend from class towed out
To the campus carnival in drag to please
Some friends. They'd cinched a skirt about

My waist, appraised me with kohl-trimmed stares,
Aimed gazes that make mirrors freckle and spot.
Soon my face was recast: crags snowed under powder
Soft as ash, brows black as a film noir plot.

By the time he sees me, at least three
People have taken me for a she. I fled
The surging, crowded room, colour flushed
From every feature that wasn't painted red.

He was always ready to fuck or fight,
Always wore an old crew neck discoloured
By his beery, unfiltered life, the muddy tone
You get from washing all your clothes in one load.

He once, as a warm-up to sex, played chess
With a woman, and then, a week later, reprised
The same game with another — her sister, no less.
He gratified a woman's sympathy, pleased

Them, I'm sure, with his indifference to physique.
He knew that when rubbed right, even cheap
Upholstery gives out a leathery shriek.
Now he feigns shock, lets his roused eyes creep

Back to mine. Then he's holding me, dancing
Me around, as if swerving from perils.
He switches to a polka, just for laughs,
Then dips me to the clink of plastic pearls.

When he pulls me up, a strap comes apart:
Hidden fibres snag, my falsies fall free.
His hand settles on some unvarnished part
And I waltz into what he makes of me.

Coming Out

Feet rush by, numbered in the thousands.
Each of us is served an oval plate of sky,
a snack, the cant and roar the twin-prop sends
to stir us as the drinks cart passes by.

People headed for weddings, funerals,
maybe, like me, mulling over what they'll say.
The ring I've never guarded, nor al-
together lost, slips off like workaday.

To fly, you must find the lift required.
And who wouldn't, propelled in this marvel
to a higher sphere, galvanic, storm-fired?
Thrust makes gains on drag, and we travel.

Then down we go, over the fall forest
that raises thrills like candy on the tongue,
red and yellow lures for the tourist:
all will be bare, once this visit's done.

In back a child calls out, "Here come the wheels!"
Shocking still, that routine shudder and hiss,
the pre-emptive hush as we cool our heels.
It had to end this way, to come to this.

Side-by-Side

For John Barton

That time all I desired fell on my shoulder,
His face a pale, soft-edged square under dark hair,
What came to be known (when I got bolder)
As "my type," had for the price of bus fare.

He slept on for miles, and I was free to stare,
To picture my hands in his fingerless gloves,
Dizzy with clothes-smell, the whiff of surplus store,
Carried away by a brief splicing of lives.

Or the plane ride, seated beside a fat,
Suited bureaucrat, still lit from the lounge,
Who lobbed jokes to colleagues a few seats back
And then fell asleep, swelling like a sponge

As sweat enough for both of us bled through
The porous spot where our arms overlapped.
His snores whirled the air, stirred the trough-
Like smells seeping from the tray on his lap.

They offered to move me, but I stayed,
To give support to this too-familiar
Person, worn by appetites I understood,
To learn what of us survives desire,

As I rested by the slumbering heap
Of him, the distance elided by sleep.

April 20

Life makes allowance for the half-lit days.
The sun rubs off the hours, penny-dull and poor.
Snail toes hid in shoes, you inch off towards
Your errand, though bones favour the cloak of home.

In this light, there is no pressing alternate, just
Walls and leaning birches to mark the bounds
Of a world gone matte. Motives speed away
Behind the one-way window of a shiny car.

Things give up their night shapes, and there's no way
To ease in by degrees. Intentions pass unnoticed.
Life's toughened at the root. The morning's
Thumbings spell a course for midday yawns.

As they edge into traffic or start to queue,
Some make extra effort at fairness.
Others flare, hoping to smoke out shadows.
And all begrudge the time for a kiss goodbye.

An uncalled-for sweater weighs on my arm.
My palm nests a garlic bulb and two limes.
Their shapes frame the season: a clutch of
Winter drifts, scoops of summer lawns gone dry.

But this is the pit of Spring, the endlessness of
Come-again. Soon things will shuck and show green.
Water joins the ruts, each path obstructed by
A platter holding branches to the sky.

A day you can manage, no fears
Of bright mornings landing a cubist's smash.
Should sun arrive and shade bloom,
Skirting trees like tossed lace:

Hold your tongue. Close your eyes and banish
The dazzle, your taste for immoderate days.

Fast-Forward

Alighting
and then gone
a fly tinted

seeming-green
cycles through
bright mica

small boil of
gold, to a
blue shiver

on the back
of my hand
spotted and

discoloured
with the scores
of seasons

past it takes
for excess
and is gone

its unnamed
smouldering
shed.

Extension I

With a wail, my sister bashed the phone,
Smashed the dial to pieces
With the receiver, like a cave dweller
Staving in skulls with a bone.

It had just begun to seem more at home.
With use, its unremarkable, glossy
Beige casing had taken on
Complex, parchment-like hues:

Patches bleached by the slow burn
Of sun, ballpoint ticks as if someone
Were keeping score, the dim halo
That pointed fingers had worn.

For years it relayed, word-for-word,
Tough exchanges and wearing appeals
And kept its grip on the wall, only to be
Dashed by her fury at not being heard.

I lived with both its limitations and mine,
Waiting for the dial to unwind,
For the numbers to slowly gurgle out. Who cared
If it improved upon the old party line

When other homes could afford all
Those rows of sleek, speedy buttons?
(You could even punch out a tune,
Though God knows who you'd call.)

The devices I craved surpassed utility.
Supine, I'd cradle a Princess phone
That ladled out intimate earfuls, imbued
My pillowed whispers with felicity,

Limbs looking slick in its pastel glow.
I got a push-button once I moved
To the city, gave up pulse and connected
Using curt, cutting-edge tone.

Still, blaring recall drilled through the air
That time I heard an old desk set ring.
Old tones of want and rage resounded,
Swamping the tended lawns of Pointe-Claire.

Silver, not beige, not on the wall, but near,
My phone trills and I press it close to hear
Voices that ache and affirm, like a phantom limb,
News that comes like a bang on the ear.

Extension II

I remember the thrill when I first strode
From room to room (even out on the step!)
Au naturel, with my new cordless phone,
How freely I engaged in hands-free mode.

Those feats now long since outstripped
By freedoms won by the cellphone crowd.
Talk walks past me, waggling and stark,
While I just sit there, tight-lipped.

Limitless reach is worth, I'm sure,
Misunderstandings when reception's poor.
But I prefer to know that somewhere
I'm joined to a wall and the line's secure.

Near the heart of the new breed sits a chip
That imperfectly mimics an antique ringer.
It can play a hives' worth of buzzes or
Trumpet a theme for the day from your hip.

Now that we're nothing but codes and hard wiring
(Though it takes a lifetime to puzzle us out),
Soon pocket-sized gadgets may carry our souls
Transmitting with digits each synapse firing.

Each generation shakes loose of a tether.
In places they've gone and buried the wires:
No clutter of birds or dangling shoes,
The space above us reverting to ether.

Window Dressing

For David Roop

From basement storage he arrives,
In forms not taken up by myth:
With his head atop a mass of silk leaves,
Or his middle joined to a mammoth

Plush bear or horses from a carousel.
With a huff (it's late, he's out-of-shape),
He loads the gap between glass and wall
With props and books culled from the shop.

His scenes eschew the unforeseen:
In spring, green crêpe sprouts on cue.
Titanic, sequined flakes of snow sail in
As soon as the pumpkins roll from view.

To avoid monotonous piles of books,
Without things getting too strange or costly,
He tries them on wall mounts, in plastic crooks,
On fish-line trapezes, but mostly

Builds towers, shelving given height
By bricks, boosted into sight-
Lines, a ziggurat rising rung by rung:
Like Babel's terraces
Hushed to a single tongue.
He works upwards,
Tips, topples, and shuffles, word-
Lessly arranges, re-arranges,
Wedding apples to oranges,
No genre gets preference:
Fiction tiered with Reference,

Paperback against a tome,
Comic strips nested
With House and Home.
Colour, dimension
Forge a relation
That, at least
For a glance's duration,
Is true.

Behind it all, panels he's recovered
With fashionable prints, a colour code
Pulsing with motif, static boundaries
That belie an optic undertow,

A drift that rouses the imperishable
Leaves, adds shimmer to lacquered rind
Ripened in the tick of incandescence.
With looking, the frame drops out of mind.

Working into the night,
His now-aching arms rise
From wick-silky sleeves, showing
The aged hatch of box-cutter slips,
Pale buttons of scars left by hot glue,
A hide fashioned from years of make-do.
No arrangement lasts, but still
He takes pains for effect.

If the job's done right, he jokes,
You'll find his work in ruin.
Someone plucks a single copy
From the pediment, cheapens
Things and asks the cost
(Often it's the props they'll
Want — they aren't for sale)

And whatever was achieved is lost,
All for a need that could be filled
By fishing through the bargain bin.

If they were something you could buy,
He'd gather up your disparate parts,
And pose them lightly on
Skewed internal furniture, turn
Crude habit into drape. Arrange you
So people stare when they pass:
A self to keep at home, behind glass.

Part 2

Black Box Blues

Your blue box is hungry for juice cartons, juice boxes, foil, aluminum
trays, and aluminum cans... Your black box is hungry for white office
and computer paper.
            — City of Ottawa 2008-2009 Collection Calendar

You rinse containers, hands bathed
in wasted water, and feel inadequate
(don't think of zealots, crushing cans),

tamp down politicos' faces, snug under
headlines or a starlet's thonged ass.
Report: unplanned trips use twice as much gas.

Yet some days you fold
tissue boxes and think you're pushing
it, heavy with the piss you hold
to avoid repeated flushing.

Compostable matter sticks
to its bucket like mud,
like the mind clings to times
when warming weather was
merely an adjunct to mood,

or else it's flung: to a future when, framed in
windows cut from re-purposed tin
your children's children leave the sky,
lift a middle finger to Earth's occluded, evil eye.

Early Reports

Got up, went ambulance chasing
for the second time this week.
Is it the failed journalist in me
that sets off down the road
to a fire and a shooting, or
the poet free to go out
on Saturdays or weekday afternoons,
eager to report a nuance?

First there's smoke over the neighbours',
thick shifting cords of black and grey
that will unseat a local landmark
by day's end. A few blocks farther and I see
drumming flames heave skyward.
A pub, shops, and apartment homes, gone.

Later on, a trip takes me past
the office where a gunman
shot five dead. I'm told reporters waited
while a ragged file ran to safety,
broke free of the complex
with eyes of the wild,
through a swamp, what's left
of the woods, up a steep rise to the road.
They joked about high heels and good suits:
a tame reflex needed to survive
assassins or a desk job, to clear
the mud of a ruined season.

Now yellow tape marks a corner of the lot,
arrests the scene itself,
while the pain and shock drain off
in a steady stream of analysis.

The paper and TV news wind us
up to the minute, bring it all home.
Something deep inside is startled,
and something, deeper still, is not.
Images that are more than scenes
(but a few senses short of suffering)
reach us in the sanctity of distance.
Not much remains to remind you
how you keep from not caring at all.

Verse seems helpless, a place to find
little more than the measurements
of a poet's heart, reflections on a flower
arched like a priestess, or leaves traced
in the palm of a newborn child,
all the significance roiling
out the backyard: a small, laminate
world, ready to pin on a knapsack flap,
nothing so big it can't be popped
right into your mouth and sucked.

There's so much fire out there —
enough to burn through every gradation
and knock war off the front page —
and blood to rinse out the soot smell.

I pass the site of the fire again and again,
through the salvage, the boarding up
and demolition. The ground churns
with rocks, the old foundation, its swells
tamped down to a parking lot.

If it's a turning, the gyre collapsing,
I've no sense of it. Each image takes our drift
without hope of suture. An end would see
the sun stopped in its course and us
seared in place: true world, shadow-robbed,
land of ashes, its stones singing fire.

Tempted

Noon, and the towers empty in one great flush.
On the streets, the shudder of the collective
rush to do lunch runs into the gutters.
Unstalked, the office animal bares hunger.

They come in odd pairs: office matron tows
network geek, fashionista heads a line
of clerks in chinos. In innocence
or full knowledge, we all must eat.

Among the mob, tireless tee shirt advocates
model bottle shapes, bodies that can
pluck me in the crowd and smack me keen.
Nothing in the day is as declarative:

consonant bones framing the scoop of chest,
biceps like two licks of cream, akimbo arms
hooked to the waist. To be tempted is not
a kingdom on offer, it's a world to behold.

The itch of potential lives in the knit
of sunny days. Sidewalk sales get brisk,
the hot dog vendor is flush with steam.
A glance lets loose a torrent in the eye.

But still we tire of particulars, living sprung
from the moment. Keep to what you know
and the rest will pass, a lost reflection
tripping down glass that panels the street.

The pool will not give up its surface.

Even drops robbed from today's plenitude go
unnoticed, back at your desk, drawing hearts
on the corner, the eyes you'll never meet.

Place Royale

Empty, still, uninviting, the park
Hushed us by design. We'd arrived too late.
Everyone had gone, turned tail in the dark
And left us morning like a licked-clean plate.

Near the sputtering fountain, we find chairs
Sitting in twos or threes or more, spread out
Un-uniformly, like bare-legged players.
Their poses revive what life was about

Last night, how people sat alone or knocked
Knees. We catch the angles where bodies met,
How folks laughed, touched, or argued as they talked,
The coarse tales sketched in the sand at their feet.

Uphill at Sacré-Coeur, chairs sit in rows
Beneath the dome that tops the city's brow.
Whispers thread the silence on the floor below,
Snapped by the creak when a body sits down.

Overheard

Running along beside us, the neighbours' lot
Has settled in its lapse. The back roof bows,
Sheds shingles. The lawn's grown up from blown seed.

Maybe a trace of care remains in the mess of branches,
Vines, and metal scrap out back. It's all past, anyway.
With his cane the remaining mobile occupant

Swipes at a weed, then turns from its bristled stare.
He's reached his limit: the buckled edge
Of driveway and the last sight of earth before

All is lost in the crowds of peonies,
Their juicy orange and white heads knocking together
Over a dark sea of leaves, pressuring the fence.

With his wife he's always spotted side-by-side
On the porch swing in most weather, morning through evening,
Their tiny, bottled voices persisting when the light goes.

That was before. We realize they've gone missing
After days, could be weeks, of no attention paid.
All night an inner room soaks in discoloured light.

The place is sold and most recently houses
An affable, tense divorcee, owner of a black Jetta and
A dog that strains to piss on the property's four corners.

From what we've seen, the house will go,
Flattened under the slightest rise in the market,
No doubt. But we've heard nothing more.

Unless you count the chimes left behind:
Hung out of easy reach, still stringing
Sound over time, a jangle that lives in our walls.

Playoffs

I asked him to please move the truck:
Its grey on greyer panels plastered
With sports fan huzzas traced in red.
The letters carouse down the side to collapse
At the fender in a barely legible pile.

Write "GO, GO, GO!" and something has to give.
In this case, the sunroof, tailgate, and hubcaps,
The rusty door smeared with a porridge of patching.

On the dash, a dayglo-skirted hula girl
Waves from her glassy habitat.
Deaf to slogans, her stencilled eyes
Stare down the road she takes unblinking
As a surge of ignition makes her shimmy.

He's profiled in the paper as an ultimate fan,
A spirit that growls and rolls down the street.

Inspiring honks and occasional shouts,
He leaves a trail of raucous belief.

I asked him to move to make room for
Unlikely arrivals. I imagine them stepping amazed
To the asphalt: dressed in robes, moving in slow orbits,
Their beautiful, soft speech praising the other team.

How to Trim Squid

After instructions included in an issue of Canadian House and Home

I understand now that what I got was
Whole squid, the kind with heads on,
Requiring me to twist the top part off
While pulling out the internal organs,

To cut off the tentacles, and discard
The hard bony bit that was attached
(The rest, at least, was good for cooking),
Peel off and discard, too, the spotted membrane
(Or "skin") on the outside of the body.

All I really wanted was the body,
A hollow, white, rubbery tube,
Bagged and delivered into clean hands:
Nothing more to do than slice it
Into rings and follow the recipe.

Suits

Laid out on the bed, sloughing plastic,
Are the clothes we've rented down to the shoes:
Inky castings of the requisite forms
That endorse at the neck with a scribble of bow.

In the catalogue they had some polish.
On receipt, we get two black shovelfuls
Sapped by hundreds of previous aspirants
Abristle with a sense of occasion.

Just what you'd expect from goods
Shipped overnight from Montreal.
Sad as rags long before midnight, thin
As the credit card slips their lease entailed.

And putting one on, I gain no substance.
The coat's best shouldered by a mannequin.
It saddles me with atmospheres,
Cuffs and yoke flagging my lack of heft.

Our hostess arrives, brisk and appalling
In the cosmetic layer she's applied
To deflect the scorch of flashes, minding
The images that will outlast her.

Slow as a beast, I stand as I'm called. The dame and
A man who shows too much sock take my hand,
Speak a word, and then move on, pausing for
Warm conversation further down the line.

Concession

For Anita Lahey

The day had been painless, the heat at its heart
Deferred by a constant breeze. A chatty, restless
Froth of people filled the park where you
Were side-show to arts and crafts.

Anyone could pick from the jar crammed
With slips, plain sheets you'd scissored to ribbons
Then inscribed with polite, handwritten replies
That thanked us for trying or gave out a prize.

Ignoring the weather, you'd bottled things up, the mass
Of losing tickets crowding the winners from sight,
And left hat and sunscreen on the table, among
Blank scraps that waited for more telling tales you'd write.

Only later, with the day's expected high settled
In my clothes, through the fuss and posture of a party
Was I told you're looking for an apartment
Without him. Then I could see how our talk

Had been pinched, caught in tidy, social forms
So easily abused. But how I need
That noise we make, to hear a sound above
The inner voice that fills the day with elegies.

Worried about sunburn, I had checked your neck
With a gentle finger press, sure that blood
Would rise and flood that tiny, pale moon.
But I saw no tinge, and left.

Maybe you planned to tell, or will never say.
The next day, you report the sting came later,
Once the fortune cookie kindnesses were scattered,
And you went home, fingers cool on the empty jar.

A Year Away

Once she chose not to sell the place
Her preparations seemed like subterfuge.
The "to do" list read like advice
For those who make leaving a refuge:

Find a couple to rent (she's pregnant —
No doubt they'd be happy to buy),
Send the near-deaf dog somewhere distant
Where she'll have room to roam and die.

Sort clothing and furniture by degrees,
Measure them daily for what they provide,
If they will suit, chafe with change, or please
In a home she's yet to step inside.

For months, life is unrelieved of larger schemes,
Its profligate categories curbed to three:
What's for storage, what comes with, and what seems
Better off shed from who and where she'll be.

What's culled she arranges on tables outside:
Lamps and appliances wrapped in their cords,
Instruments half-learned, then set aside,
Racquets, pads, and helmets that record

Every sport her son grew bored of and quit.
The glassware, milky, tinted, or clear,
Its shelf dust blown away, is sunlit,
Shines with disuse, brimming with air.

Cars pull over, people stop in twos and threes,
Until it's near-impossible to pass through
The crowd of strangers who assess what she's
Willing to disown for a buck or two.

She coaxes, tells stories that might revive
The object's charm, what compelled her to buy,
Lights a lamp as they hold it with a live
Extension to kindle its dormant chemistry.

The day he left, her boyfriend hugged my daughter
Out front, framed by the tidy flower beds,
Standing in sock feet and shaking with laughter,
As if his shoes, not him, were flying ahead.

One day left. She strains to clean
The windshield of the old, dented sedan
Before its new owners arrive, and explains
That she loves it, would buy it back again:

Something I never would have guessed.
Now, so much of hers is gone for good
And nothing's certain till the year is past.
Absence settles down in the neighbourhood.

Her garden grows in ways she can't prevent,
Undeterred by rumours of return we've heard,
While she takes a bulb, inhales its scent,
And plants it in the soil of Oxford.

When Someone Suggested Poker

Not a spike but a slow, easy sweetening
To a boom in the lunchroom atmosphere.
The men making sport of the premise
(The woman among them content to spear

Bits of salad in silence) their words thrown
Over tables, bodies swivelling to reply
From tipped-back chairs, being careful to sluice
The talk with jokes, bicker on the rules of play.

And the rest of us: animals come to water,
Accustomed to rustles from the bushes,
We heat up small, vented bowls, pry meals
From icy cardboard, or pace the line

Of windows that would be seen down a hall
In a Sirk melodrama, or else raised up
To the roof so the high light could fall
Around us in Technicolor fronds and blushes.

But the tables kept their usual arrangements,
And we got sorted, took our routes and soon
Carried on, voices mazed in cubicles,
Diminished in the frames of afternoon.

When We Say

Say green, meaning grass, tending to
a gist that thrives to exclusion:
age-old fresh patch slides under sneakers,
the reach of imagined fairway.

But at grass level, little land of grass,
things are often spotty, or blackened,
or watery with shine: stopped short or frayed
from holding out, the delicate ribbing gone dun.

Hear the whispers crowding when you say green:
The fielding of the ground you walk on.

Part 3

Evolution

Every parent has a limit: these days
they've drawn the line at gaining weight,
given us jogging strollers, baby boot camp.
Unlike our mothers, who followed regimens
older than the Stoics: sneaking bites
of raw potato, meats, and cookie dough,
as if each taste was test for poison.
In a blink, they'd down the scraps
from plates, refusing to face the waste.

As burdens mounted, they recouped
esteem with a plate of squares
that never failed to please. They adapted,
tucked swelling thighs and breasts inside
some off-the-rack support, spared
themselves the room to jiggle and chafe.

At the table end or farther still,
Father smoked like an autumnal fire,
almost quenched with beer
or work-exhausted. Scarce heat
enough to warm small hands or cheeks.

After those dinners, we'd never again
hunger for family. No questions asked,
each parent-pod distilled
something warm and buttery
under the skin, and we fed.

Spring Snow

Our Sunday's rescued from routine by boys
who commandeer the couch upstairs, wrestle
with the remote and each other. The row will
end when the fair one hits pause and obeys.
They watch as a grown man takes for his sun
a pumpkin, an apple for our green globe,
and moves the smaller fruit to make an ad lib
orbit. He tips it, and the seasons run.

Below, adults assay the family model
over shifting, sticky plates and heated talk
that leaves the coffee cold. What to tick
off when love ends? The law's a homily:
show cruelty, adultery, or time apart,
and you've got grounds. Legal settlement
robs native feeling of entitlement,
a freeze that broaches the equatorial heart.

The kids run out into a day that calls
them kings. They're castled on piles growing fat
with snow, halfway to water as it falls.
Winter heaped it on. Light holds the eye fast.
"It's the best stuff for snowmen and snowballs,"
C. says, "and the kind least likely to last."

Sea Goddess

1

That's my Exhibit A, out on display.
Clearly pissed, if a stone could seethe.
She sits semi-coiled, torso in mounds
like a clump of dung: *Sedna with Hairbrush*.

Tough subject, a loss-pained deity
who turns bounty on and off, like a tap.
Some artist with cheek devised
the telling marks we recognize:
swirls for eyes and teats, a pouting lip,
fishtail in outline, scalp a fright of fur
that vents her anger into the air.

And in hand, what soothes her age-old
troubles. Under the brush, she finds peace,
forgets that life unspools into tangle and misery,
the day she woke on an island couched
in promise, love forgone while
her bird-spouse feared all but flight.

Her father's rescue foundered. To rid himself
he dumped her, chopped her grip to slaughter
as she clung to the boat: bits that sunk and stewed,
became a brood that stocks the sea. Every hunter since
prays for seals to finger the water's seam
for breath, sees in tusks a twist of nail.
At her pleasure, the icy, pent-up waters teem,
her children arriving from deep dissolution.

2

Of course, I've added ripples to her story,
colourings that make her current,
just as she enlivens me and mine.
Like when I take the pleasure of my mother,
taboo I break behind the bathroom door
cast in the water's shallow, silver moods.

She'd often claim the bather's right
to not reply when called, a single
mother immersed in passing respite.
I'd still burst in, throw my questions clear
before I was sunk for breath (my sister,
so casual, sat on the toilet and talked)
for seeing the wildness above her thighs,
too bushy for such a well-manicured soul,
the stretch marks in pearl blues
that laurelled her belly, her navel blossom
perched like an inward-listening ear.

She wondered on the peace we stormed,
content to starve us, for a while at least,
half-listening to beseeching voices
reaching to a scream: for a moment,
an answer to her hopeless case,
to hear us rising to the bait.

The Balloon

The era of the Giant Floating Fish
Of Great Happiness began with a knot
That tied it to my daughter's wrist.
The slender tether went loose, then taut,

As it ducked small troubles in the air.
In a flash we lost what insulates
A soul from delight, and marched out to where
The day paraded, past the parking lots,

Past the smiling, upward-pointing people
Who cheered the puffed-out torso, tail, and fin,
Its docile drift of gold, pink, and purple,
That she compelled with a spell of ribbon.

Its filmy skin had crackled, otherwise
We heard no complaint over the tank's wild
Exhalation as it rose in our eyes,
Becoming lighter, more empty, it seemed, as it filled.

Now it's home, loosed into the ceiling's pool
Where it nibbles at corners, nodding to
A Handel air, a-bob like an apple
For sing-along songs or a piano tune.

Each day it loses shape, gas in traces
Dissolving in confluent shouts and laughter:
Soft, sinking to the floor's dry spaces,
Watching us rise, as it submerges under air.

Lessons from Horus

By lesson three, we've come to expect it:
that after we've followed him into the pool,
and the babies go light and slippery in our arms,
our teenage instructor, name of Horus,

will tell us to practise back floats and then
wander off, to tumble from the pool edge
or try to sink the turtle mat, each leap
enraging the water, thrusting waves our way.

The children smile, ready to drown, to try
the sweet immersion that lies beyond our reach.
They clap as he sinks, laugh when he rises unblinking,
hair washed forward like a greased, black wing.

We no longer wait for correction or praise,
but choose to ignore, or improvise, or start over,
persisting with encouragements in a pitch
that's cued to excitement or imminent loss.

When time's almost up, he returns and demands
we run in a circle, increasing the pace until
the group surges like a twelve-headed dervish,
legs trembling, two dozen eyes blinking in the spray.

At the threshold of a secret purpose
he calls a stop, then falls and floats:
stares upward in silence as we dry off,
riding the current that's left behind.

Sugar Bowl

With a liquid smack, the piñata bursts spilling
Candy, like a puking, tattered flower.

The boy keeps lunging, bashing again and again,
His boxers riding up in back, neat as a folded sheet.

Children comb the grass, the sweating earth,
Then scatter, hands filled from the confusion.

Each twice-wrapped package holds a diversion,
A bit of spun syrup, the colour and shape of

Bite-sized ham and eggs, a little burger with cheese,
Or a row of crooked, greenish teeth in foul gums.

They bring them to us to open and we do,
Telling them to wait, to save some, it will keep:

Not to stick a wetted finger in the bowl.

Room for More

A second child adds nothing new
To days spent wiping at crusted glue
And glitter, hanging up to dry
Onesies pulled from the hamper's high tide.

A second child, like a life past halfway,
Spares us high hopes, gratifies delay.
Spooning out to the first, her sister heard
Griping on your lap, you talk of a third.

The Performance

Cheap puppet, a limp-limbed, strung-up doll
hangs between the man and a child of three:
a toy conductor, pitched and tossed in a squall
of up-and-down tugs, roughly rhythmic at best.

In another age, a craftsman might have
tuned his joints, added more strings and the ease
of a sidestep, or tooled the fused fingers
to move with wit, like hopping chickadees.

Soft stuff might have ringed his head instead
of the grey, synthetic tufts that stand
unruffled while he's jerked to match each
bash of cymbals rolling from the stereo.

The flood of years has nearly washed
the maestro from our muddled store of types.
His baton, downsized, wobbles butt to tip,
keeping tempo with the dabbling hands above.

After work, the day's small indignities,
the puppeter's jacket lies folded on the couch
peeled from the pushed-up sleeves that bunch
like a swami's pants above his labouring arms.

Even at play, his worth needs affirming:
It bares the need that's hid in the stuffing.
The girl should laugh, chime with the quick in him,
cheer on what he's made from next to nothing.

Off to the side, the woman he lives with,
who watched him rehearse and knows his looks,
freshens her laughter, thinks about clapping,
as his words coax, growing sharp as hooks.

Unsmiling, the girl waits for her turn at things,
thinks how he'll dance when she holds the strings.

The Chaperone

The wagon's metals grate, as if
to protest the use that's made of it
by five children:

One pulls, two ride,
and two more run alongside,
baby sitting neatly in
the preschooler's spread-legged "V".

It bears this restive weight
for each new generation,
always wakes to find fresh tremors
knocking in its wood.

They're in charge of where
we're headed, lead you and me
through summer warmth
that's lasted to Thanksgiving.

It's easy going, the after-dinner pace
quickened by the pavement
of a new suburb, in the
smooth sameness that reigns
before each lot becomes distinct.

I lag behind, worried by
the question you might think to ask,
and puzzle as a stranger might,
sorting out which kids are kin.

No word is needed for the twins'
resemblance, or the boy

you'd guess their cousin,
so often is he seen in tow.

Which leaves my daughters,
not related in a legal sense,
but still they're factors
in the holiday equation.

Telling more would set apart
my oldest, rely on
patterns spied in blood:

Talk I stall, before it's drawn
into adoption's pained mechanics.
It can't be done in passing.

A few steps back keeps me near
enough, to tie a lace or set to rights
the creaking, weathered invention,
to where I see their well-paired traits,
discern born sisters
in beauty, smarts, and speed.

The children drop the wagon
and break into a run, ply their
zigzag, bobbing weave through
the park's bright geometry.

Absorbed in play they fade
in the tick and spill of dark.
They are the clocks. Here's a bench.
We can sit and watch while I explain.

Part 4

From the Couch

When will you stop
Making noise in the kitchen?

Time scurries by, unwatched.
Now you take up something metal,

Producing another sharp, clean
Rent in my mind's plush hermitage.

I'm baited by the singular silence
That rests beyond collisions at the sink,

The sundering union of pot and lid.
I think of the nothing that, once ingested,

Calms the shooting pulse: of leaping free,
Toes uncurled, into the arc of completed thought.

I think how well I will speak of you
When you are gone.

In the Underworld

Vagaries of weather add coats
to the rack, weighing down confidence
in warmer days to come. We stew
In heated rooms and itch for winter's ruin.

On the lawn, the crest of two March storms
subsides. Heat is creeping,
turns crystal to vapour, even though
the nights are freezing or below.

This year we got to Spring by plane,
pocketed coatless days under
the plate of London sky, its scenes
of bone and blue in slow rotation.

By Tube, we follow heaven's light,
focused and fractured for the stage,
and sit in the upmost circle, waiting
for the dancing heart of Gluck's *Orfeo*.

But the ache for the familiar
is quenched by surprise as
our blessed spirits skip the frolic
and execute a stately nude pavane.

These shades shift the focus, portray
the reduction of limb and sex to a daub
on the canvas of this bare stage, this life,
in their charmed circles of repose.

The lovers stand outside, amid debris
that does duty as both graveyard and spots
Elysian, and act out Love's proviso:
look away, don't touch, just be on your way.

In song they tear their bond to pieces,
dress it in the farthest thing from love,
and plead the best intentions
when what goes around comes back.

And in the separation, a stillness,
as tick-tock players turn.
A face turns, a hand's held out:
Equivocation of the zero heart.

God's intervention reunites them,
though they brave a heat like hell,
And we recover in the time it takes
to zip up a fleece or nylon shell.

Beyond the Furies is a river
travelling swiftly past remembering
that carries us to higher ground, happy
in jackets, adrift on Spring's low boil.

Polymer

Those who desire an exceptionally strong bond
Should consider epoxy cement. Use it

To fix a shoe heel and the mend
Will carry on and on underfoot,

To secure a precious stone and never fear
It will slip from its setting.

To mend a doll's face, its chippy hands,
To join breaks into lasting fissures.

Most brands are sold in pairs of tubes
Whose contents you blend in equal parts:

Use a toothpick or the tiny plastic
Rapier found under each lid.

The mixture heats up, then cools to a solid
Substance that can't be molded, won't melt.

If, in error, one tube is parted from its mate
(at the factory, or in typical household clutter)

And gets squeezed out on its own,
We've seen how it goes:

The adhesive thin and weepy, endlessly tacky, or
Thick with dust until it's finally wiped away;

The hardener going stale, with nothing to cure,
Attempting to marry the unavailable air.

Apogee with Coffee

I can reach my office cubicle two ways:
Escalator to the mezzanine, then hop
On the elevator, or elevator non-stop.
Either path works fine if my day's

A bit rushed, but neither gets me fresh air,
Something to look at, or promotes ecology,
And in terms of brute physiology
My heart works no harder to get me there.

I'm left to match metaphor to my ascension:
Mixed modes (a hint to a clambering rise)
Or a rocketing up into fluorescent skies?
A morning stalled in a fog of intention.

The thought-thicket parts as I split hairs.
I remember how we met: on the stairs.

Twice That Day

There's no escaping the bliss cycle:
Just hours out of bed and we fall back in.
Sundays are for slow cooking and sex
That ups the ante from Friday's artless rub.

The bite is empty, still something's fed
as the unlooked-for boils up through
the toss and jumble. Given time,
low heat catches the flash of flame.

In the kitchen, a medley in the making
catches my ear, plays on elements:
Foam shuffles in the pot, implements chime,
green garnishes the tomato's rose.

My hands reap tones for the nose.
My fingers trick your ear, dip where
your spine flowers, like a hum-drunk bee.
We feast on what we espouse.

The chili pot joins aromas we throw:
Oil tucked under a nail, knuckles laced.
First time, garlic and onion, an acid whiff.
Second time, perfume, sweet cilantro.

Hearing Pan

So the way we did it was this: he'd work out the steps with me —
the Continental or whatever — then, having played Ginger to Fred,
I would then go off, the dance all ready in my mind and then be
Fred to Ginger.

— Hermes Pan

Weeks before film sees light
The two men polish the dance to routine.
Cheek-to-cheek, they rehearse until late,

Cobbling the steps she'll dance in, tighten
Each arc for an absent gown's sweep.
Stumbling in on Fred and Pan, the crew would lighten

Their shock with a joke, shout "sorry" and keep
Backing away from those queer, uncostumed poses:
Pan bent like a starlet, but his time came cheap.

When light pours on the stage, the camera closes
In to show he holds her no closer than Pan,
A space they cradle, a bright egg of ache, that loses

Nothing in translation as she falls upon
His circling arm, braced for a man's weight,
Her eyes catching the violet ebb of her spin.

Their passage leaves a limelight rub, a trace of what
Compelled them, in the grain of the late-late show
That watching shades drink in, down to the last watt.

His foot sounds are dubbed in later, so
You're seeing Ginger, but hearing Pan,
A dark, cunning rap that grounds her glow.

Like wings that lighten the feet, it happens,
And we can't put off the tap-tap invitation
To step onto the dark, empty floor and begin.

Part dazzle, part thievery, the carnal imitation
Of pale feathers blooming, the stiff collar pointed,
Or black silk, wetted to a "barely there" sensation.

For us no sleight of sound and light, instead
The sight and warmth of the chosen mate,
Dancing, duplicitous: a little Ginger, a little Fred.

The Blanket

The label reads: 100 % UNDETERMINED FIBRES.
Like everything kept in the upstairs closet, wedged in
Among the tilting, mismatched strata of our pasts combined,
It's of unknown provenance, its value ripe for dispute.

Eerily weightless, it will not lie flat, makes you imagine
The rounds and pockets hide sloughed pyjamas,
Ambulant pillows, balled-up animals, or some other body lost
   in sleep.
Its colour resolves, on staring, to a purplish blue-grey,

Like a pointillist rendering of a soiled pigeon on a dull day.
In short, a blanket of nothing so much as vulcanized lint
Bought from (and possibly made of) Canadian Tire,
Forged when a nation's aspirations rested on miracle fibres,

A vestige made of tail-ends, waste, god knows what else.
Lie under it, and the heat that builds to something scorching
Is all your own. What you give off, just walking around, is
Thrown back, until you're swamped, broiled hot as shame.

But if I'm tired, I don't care. I pull it down and over me.
And somewhere in sleep's plush furnace the mind
Pulls strands, indiscriminate, the day's weave
Is laced with the shimmer of limitless unknowing:

The sleep that blanket brings is unnatural and deep.
Sometimes I've left it out, and you've succumbed.
I see it on the bed, arched in a curve borrowed
From your spine. As if it, too, expected to rise and go.

Acknowledgements

I would like to thank John Barton, Jeffery Donaldson, Anita Lahey, Missy Marston, and Molly Peacock for their comments and suggestions during the writing and revision of these poems.

Some poems in this collection (in earlier forms) appeared in *Arc, Canadian Notes & Queries, The Fiddlehead, Literary Review of Canada, The Malahat Review, ottawater,* and *Queen's Quarterly.*

"Place Royale" was included in *Seminal: The Anthology of Canadian Gay Male Poetry*; and "The Blanket," in *The Best Canadian Poetry in English 2008.*